O Jerusalem

BY JANE YOLEN

ILLUSTRATED BY
JOHN THOMPSON

THE BLUE SKY PRESS

AN IMPRINT OF SCHOLASTIC INC. · NEW YORK

To Norman and Zane Kotker,
with loving thanks.
J.Y.

To my Mom and Dad—
thanks for all your love and support.
J.M.T.

Jerusalem is a place unlike any other — a holy city for three major religions.
Because the city has evoked so many rich associations and feelings throughout
history, no single presentation of Jerusalem can be definitive. We hope this book
will serve as a point of departure for discussion about this fascinating place,
which endures as a vibrant city and a living symbol. We gratefully acknowledge
the invaluable assistance provided by Dr. Lawrence Schiffman, Professor of Hebrew
and Judaic Studies, New York University; Rev. Orlanda Brugnola, Faculty,
Department of Art, Music, and Philosophy, John Jay College of Criminal Justice;
and Dr. Peter Awn, Professor of Islamic Studies, Columbia University.

Special thanks to Tim Peck, who asked for this book,
and to Lauren Thompson, for her sharp eye and loving attention to detail.

THE BLUE SKY PRESS

Text copyright © 1996 by Jane Yolen
Illustrations copyright © 1996 by John Thompson
All rights reserved.
Library of Congress Cataloging-in-Publication Data
Yolen, Jane.
O Jerusalem / by Jane Yolen; illustrated by John Thompson.
p. cm.
Summary: A poetic tribute to Jerusalem, in honor of the 3000th anniversary of its founding,
celebrating its history as a holy city for three major religions.
ISBN 0-590-48426-5
1. Jerusalem — Juvenile poetry. 2. Children's poetry, American. [1. Jerusalem — Poetry.
2. American poetry.] I. Thompson, John, 1940-   ill. II. Title.   PS3575.04303 1996
811'.54 — dc20 95-6013
CIP   AC
12 11 10 9 8 7 6 5 4 3 2 1   6 7 8 9/9 0 1/0
Printed in Singapore   First printing, April 1996
The paintings for this book were executed in
acrylic on Strathmore five-ply kid-finish bristol board.
The text type was set in Centaur, with italic in Galliard.
The calligraphy was hand-drawn by Jeanyee Wong.
Color separations were made by Bright Arts, Ltd., Singapore.
Printed and bound by Tien Wah Press, Singapore.
Production supervision by Angela Biola
Designed by Claire B. Counihan

About Jerusalem

To find the city of Jerusalem on a map of the world,
first go east from the United States, and then drop
down a bit south to the Mediterranean Sea. On the east
coast of the sea you will find a very large country called
Syria and a very small sliver marked Israel. Inland in Israel,
lying on the flank of the country of Jordan, is Jerusalem.
It sits on a ridge of the Judean hills, some two thousand
five hundred feet above the Mediterranean Sea.

Jerusalem has commanded that spot for three thousand
years and is a center of worship and a holy city for
three major world religions: Judaism, Christianity, and
Islam.

You would think that a place considered so important
to religions, and called by many the City of Peace,
would be a quiet and serene area. But in fact the city has
been fought over and fought in, and has been razed
down and built up again, by three thousand years' worth
of conquerors.

Every day, people in Jerusalem — Jews, Christians,
and Muslims — pray to God. All three groups believe
that Jerusalem should belong to them. And that is
Jerusalem's weakness — and its strength.

Seventy Thousand Angels

Angel of old petitions,
Angel of torn letters,
Angel of illuminations,
Pray for thy fold.

Angel of tattered prayer books,
Angel of worn sandals,
Watch the feet of pilgrims,
Lead them from the cold.

Angel of ancient thresholds,
Angel of Heaven's casements,
Fling wide the gates of Paradise
That Allah may behold.

According to Muslim tradition, while Allah looks down from a door in Heaven, seventy thousand angels pray nightly for the pilgrims going into Jerusalem. At first, the Muslim prophet Muhammad instructed his followers to pray toward Jerusalem as a holy place. Later he changed that to Mecca. But Jerusalem has remained for the Muslims the city of prophets, wonder workers, and angels — the place from which the living Muhammad ascended to Heaven.

Measures

Of the ten measures of beauty God gave the world,
he gave Jerusalem nine:
> the sacred hills, the soft winds,
> the wall of cries, the bowl of blue sky,
> the brooding Moriah filling men with awe,
> groves of olives bitter and sweet,
> caves where kings and kings of kings
> lay down an eternity,
> the dark-haired men talking quickly,
> the dark-eyed women walking softly —
> sons and daughters of God
> eating his words of honey
> off the teacher's slate.

"Of the ten measures of beauty given to the world, God gave Jerusalem nine" is an old rabbinical saying. But every poet counts the nine differently. Mount Moriah and the Cave (or Tomb) of Kings are sites within the greater city and are important to the religious and ethnic groups living there. In Judaism, to teach how sweet God's word is, it has sometimes been the custom to smear a young child's slate with honey for him to lick off.

Abraham's Message to the Terah Clan

This is your dowry,
O daughters of Zion:
sand and soil and rock.
This is your marriage portion,
O daughters of Jerusalem:
a city sprung from stone.
Take your flocks,
the lambs and young goats,
legs weak as willows.
Take your pockets of new dreams.
Follow the desert's pasture south
into the land of Canaan.
Strangers we will be there,
stranger still those we meet.
But we will make ourselves a home
with candle, salt, and bread,
with water and with wine.
We will lie down a family
and rise up a nation.

Considered the father of both the Jews and the Arabs (the Jews through his son Isaac, the Arabs through his son Ishmael), Abraham was of the Terah clan. Under his guidance, the clan migrated in about 2000 B.C.E. from Mesopotamia to Canaan with their flocks. There, according to God's promise, the descendants of Abraham were to become as numerous as the stars in the sky. It is thought they settled in the place we now know as Jerusalem.

King David's Tomb

Before you were dust,
You were a king.
Before you were a king,
You were a man.
Before you were a man,
You were a boy.
You had a boy's eye,
Clear as a sparrow's,
And a boy's joy
With a sling.

O David,
What if every smooth stone flung
Were somehow recalled,
Bringing back bird and hare,
Bringing back giant and wolf.
Would Jerusalem itself stand, still
Shining upon its stony seat
Among the stony hills?

According to tradition, when David was a shepherd
boy, he was so skillful with his slingshot, he could
bring down bird, hare, or wolf. Eventually he used that
slingshot to fell the mighty giant, Goliath, whose very
presence in the enemy's army seemed to guarantee that
David's people — the Hebrews — would be defeated.
For his courage and skill, the boy David was brought to
King Saul's palace and became king of Israel after him.
When King David captured Jerusalem from the Jebusites
around 1000 B.C.E., he made it the capital of his kingdom.
Under his rule, Jerusalem had its first real flowering
as a city.

Stone Upon Stone

Stone upon stone a city rises,
Stone upon stone it falls.
Man upon man each war surprises
Altars, buildings, walls.

> David,
> Solomon,
> Nebuchadnezzar,
> Maccabee,
> Herod,
> And Hadrian,
> Constantine,
> Khosrau,
> Saladin,
> And Suleiman.

This is a song we sing to conquerors,
A hymn we make to war,
The straight plumb line of rules and rulers —
That's what fighting's for.

Stone upon stone a city rises,
Stone upon stone it falls.
Man upon man each war surprises
Us all.

The list of generals and kings who have conquered and
then ruled Jerusalem over the centuries is very long. The
diverse peoples who have inhabited it make a long list,
too. So often, an army comes in, levels part of the city
during the fight, and then builds it up again. This has
been going on, stone upon stone, for three thousand years.
And still we are surprised.

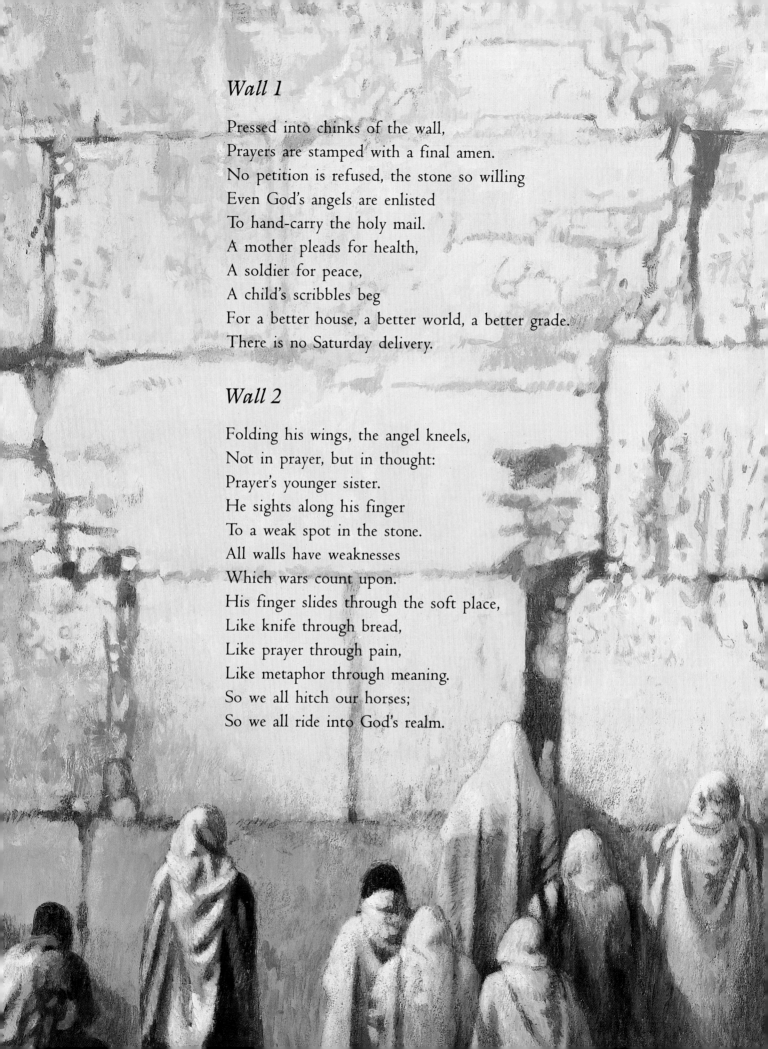

Wall 1

Pressed into chinks of the wall,
Prayers are stamped with a final amen.
No petition is refused, the stone so willing
Even God's angels are enlisted
To hand-carry the holy mail.
A mother pleads for health,
A soldier for peace,
A child's scribbles beg
For a better house, a better world, a better grade.
There is no Saturday delivery.

Wall 2

Folding his wings, the angel kneels,
Not in prayer, but in thought:
Prayer's younger sister.
He sights along his finger
To a weak spot in the stone.
All walls have weaknesses
Which wars count upon.
His finger slides through the soft place,
Like knife through bread,
Like prayer through pain,
Like metaphor through meaning.
So we all hitch our horses;
So we all ride into God's realm.

King Solomon built Jerusalem's first Temple, which was
destroyed by the invading Babylonians. A second great
Temple was built by Herod, and it was razed by the
Romans. Only part of the Second Temple's retaining
wall remains. For centuries Jews gathered along this wall
to pray and weep about their misfortunes, so it became
known by some as the Wailing Wall. Today it is considered a place of joy by many Jews, who prefer to call it
the Western Wall. By old custom, some Jews write
prayers on slips of paper and "post" them in the wall's
chinks. Saturday is the Jewish sabbath, and notes are not
left in the wall that day, nor is mail delivered. The
Muslim tradition of the wall is different. There is a
legend that the angel Gabriel poked his finger into the
wall to make a hitching post for the steed on which the
prophet Muhammad ascended to Heaven.

Dome of the Rock

Three times holy,
Three faces of God
Stare from the limestone base,
Now Christian,
Now Muslim,
Now Jew.

Jew:

If stone could weep, it would,
Crying hard tears
For a father willing to sign God's name
Across the throat of his son.

Muslim:

If stone could sigh, it would,
A thousand, thousand *du`at*
Impressing on the rock face
Beside Muhammad's footprint.

Christian:

If stone could sing, it would,
A chorus of psalms
To open the gates of Paradise
On the Day of Judgment.

Three times holy,
Three faces of God
Stare from the limestone base,
Now Christian,
Now Muslim,
Now Jew.

Now one.

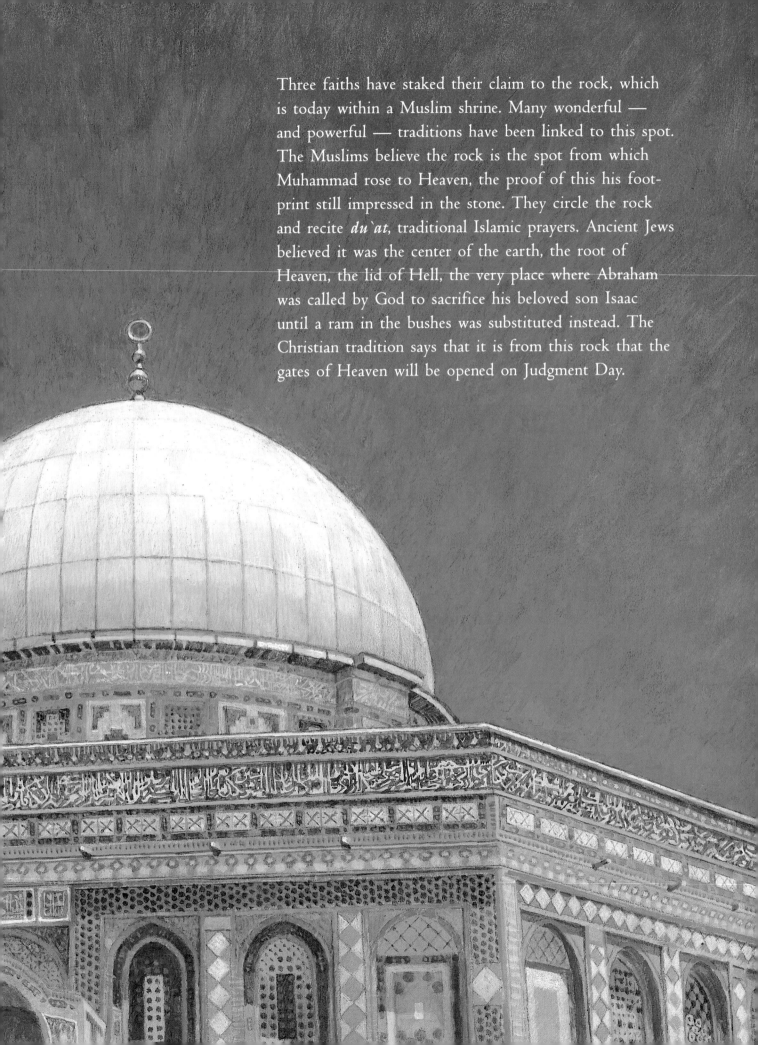

Three faiths have staked their claim to the rock, which is today within a Muslim shrine. Many wonderful — and powerful — traditions have been linked to this spot. The Muslims believe the rock is the spot from which Muhammad rose to Heaven, the proof of this his footprint still impressed in the stone. They circle the rock and recite *du`at*, traditional Islamic prayers. Ancient Jews believed it was the center of the earth, the root of Heaven, the lid of Hell, the very place where Abraham was called by God to sacrifice his beloved son Isaac until a ram in the bushes was substituted instead. The Christian tradition says that it is from this rock that the gates of Heaven will be opened on Judgment Day.

Pilgrimage

Up we come from Joppa on the rocky trail
Where raiders wait,
Final as a judgment.
Close by close we go, heartbeats apart.
I startle at a falling stone,
Another at his camel's cough.
No one speaks above a whisper;
We are silent as sand.
Who dies will be left unburied
To be hymned by jackals,
Shriven by hawks.

But Jerusalem, O Jerusalem,
You are worth the trials, the silence, the fear,
For when we come into Jerusalem,
Then God's heaven is near.

An Englishman on his way to Jerusalem on religious pilgrimage in 1102 wrote: "Saracens, always laying snares for Christians, lie hidden in the hollow places of the mountains." The word "Saracen" was a medieval European name for Muslims or Arabs. It was not a particularly nice term. For almost two hundred years, the constant wars for Jerusalem fought between Muslims and Christians meant that *all* pilgrims were in danger. Sometimes the villains were raiders like the Crusaders, sometimes they were local Arab people. It did not matter. Still the pilgrims came. The pilgrims, however, were often ill-equipped for the difficult conditions. Many died on the way. But all felt that Jerusalem was worth the danger and the fear.

Via Dolorosa

Friday is the day for walking
over the small-stepped streets
from the playground of the Arab school,
fourteen stops to the tomb.
We seal up the spaces with our prayers,
make way for passersby,
read the stone stigmata like a map.
When we come to the arch
marked ECCE HOMO,
those prayers turn solid
and halt us, heavy as a cross.
Here, indeed, is the man.

On Friday afternoons at three o'clock, the old quarter
of Jerusalem is filled with crowds of devout Christians
following the route known as the Via Dolorosa, or
Sorrowful Way, that Jesus took to the place of his
crucifixion. There are fourteen stops or "stations." The
fourth is an arch where the Roman-appointed official,
Pontius Pilate, showed Jesus to the crowd and pro-
claimed, "Behold the man!"

In the Hall of the Last Supper

Who asked the Four Questions
On that night in this hall
When the Master spoke betrayal
And broke the body's bread?

Who spoke with tongues of fire
On that night in this hall,
When the wild wind sang a Kaddish
Across the wine cup of the dead?

I spoke in Hebrew,
in Latin,
in Greek.
You spoke Aramaic.
What languages did we not speak
On that night,
In this hall,
Full of new wine,
New spirit,
All.

In the hall of David's tomb is an upstairs dining room
in which, according to tradition, Jesus and the disciples
held the Last Supper. It was a seder, a ritual meal eaten
for the Jewish festival of Passover, at which customarily
the youngest participant asks Four Questions as part of
the celebration. It was at this dinner that Jesus first
spoke of the one who would betray him. And here he
first spoke about bread being his body and wine being
his blood, which became the basis of the Christian com-
munion ceremony. Seven weeks later, the disciples again
went to the room, and a great wind suddenly filled the
house. They saw "tongues of fire" and began to speak in
many different languages. In this poem, the wind sings the
Jewish prayer for the dead — *Kaddish* — across the cup
Jesus used for the *Kiddush* — the Jewish prayer over wine.

Tombs

Everywhere the dead creep in:
into catacombs filled with chambers,
into graves deep in sandy soil,
into sarcophagi ringed with stone lions,
into clay jars and wooden casks,
into the orange-grove gardens,
into the very stone itself
where Jerusalem dreams the past.

History is a yahrzeit candle.
One terrible wind could blow it out.

Norman Kotker says, in *The Earthly Jerusalem*, that the city is "More thickly populated with the dead than the living." And, he adds, "Bones are found at almost every building site." This is not surprising for a city that has a continuous history of three thousand years, where — legend says — even Adam, the first man, is buried. In Jewish culture, a yahrzeit candle burns each year on the anniversary of a death.

Going Out Damascus Gate

Behind us the city rests on its rock,
patient as a lion.
Only the noise of the *suk* follows us,
voices sharp as claws on stone.

Why not go south to Beersheba?
Why not go east to the Dead Sea?
Why not go west to Rehovot?
Why not go north to Galilee?

We turn and re-enter Damascus Gate,
the serried arches like open jaws,
the stones like teeth.

So why go back to the belly of the beast
with all the world before us?
For in Jerusalem we will be born again,
like all children,
with blood on our heads
and a promised future before.

Built in the sixteenth century, Damascus Gate was one
of the major projects of the Ottomans, who captured
Jerusalem in 1517. Damascus Gate is the city's principal
northern entrance. *Suk* (pronounced "sook") is Arabic
for an open-air bazaar where sellers and buyers bargain
noisily over the price of wares.

Tokens from Jerusalem

If each of us takes a token stone
Smooth and round as tears;
If each of us takes a handful of earth
The color of all our fears;
If each of us fills a flask with water
Sogged as human cares
Will Jerusalem still bear the weight
Of pilgrim hopes and prayers?

It was the custom for many years for pilgrims to carry
away tokens from their trips to Jerusalem. Christians
took stones from the area around the Golden Gate.
Jewish pilgrims filled small bags with earth from the
Mount of Olives to spread on their graves, thus assuring
themselves a place in the world to come. Other pilgrims
filled flasks with water from the rivers which, they
thought, had wondrous restorative powers.

Jerusalem 3000

Here, where prayer was born,
War has finally died;
Where faith was made,
Condemned and tried,
Risen up, cast down,
Drowned in blood,
In thunder, brimstone,
Fire and in flood,
Now all children here
Walk hand in hand
Across the well-worn rocks
And shifting sand.

A thousand, thousand wars
Can take their toll.
Blood stains each rock
And every soul.
But O Jerusalem,
Your promise is kept
That peace shall one day reign
As long as we once wept.
We celebrate this year
When all wars finally cease:
Jerusalem on Earth
and Earth in peace.

"City of Peace" is one of the seventy names given
Jerusalem by rabbinical tradition. Perhaps in the year
3000 peace will finally come to Jerusalem.

Afterword

I visited Jerusalem a long time ago, in 1966. I did not see any spilled blood. What I saw were stones and people.

There were stone houses, stone holy places, stone synagogues and mosques and churches, stone gates, stone pathways, stone steps, cobbled roads, and in the fields, as if they were growing there, more stones. Much of the stone is Jerusalem limestone, the color of honey, the color of earth.

The people were more diverse: *sabras* or native Israelis, in their shorts; Hasidic men with their black hats and long black coats, beards and side curls; Jewish men in skullcaps; Israeli soldiers carrying *uzis*, submachine guns; Muslim men in checked headdresses; Muslim women covered entirely except for their eyes; monks in brown habits; nuns in black dresses; priests whose white collars marked them out. And of course, because Jerusalem is an international city, there were tourists from many countries loaded down with cameras of every shape and size.

Stones and people. I did not see any blood — though a few weeks after I left Jerusalem, there was another war there. There have been a number since.

Perhaps by the celebration of Jerusalem's *next* great birthday there will only be stones and people. Perhaps by then the spilling of blood in the name of the City of Peace will — at last — be at an end.

— *Jane Yolen*